Key Stage 2 English Creative Writing

WORKBOOK **1**

Short Story Writing

Dr Stephen C Curran

Edited by Andrea Richardson

This book belongs to

Accelerated Education Publications Ltd

Contents

Chapter One
Starting Points
1. The Five Senses

Human beings receive information from the world around them through the **Five Senses**. These senses could be called the 'gateways to the soul' because they are the means by which we connect with the inner person. They are as follows:

Sight • Hearing • Touch • Smell • Taste

Exercise 1: 1 Try this experiment to engage two of your senses right now.

1) Look around you, where you are right now, and see if you notice one thing you have not seen before. ________________
2) Close your eyes right now and listen for one sound you have not heard before in the space you are in. ______________

Every day our senses receive huge amounts of information. Successful writing involves being able to use and organise this information creatively. It is important to think about our experiences and the information we receive through each sense.

Exercise 1: 2 List things you have experienced today through each sense.

Today I have seen: e.g. a car

1. _______________ 2. _______________ 3. _______________

Today I have heard: e.g. an aeroplane

1. _______________ 2. _______________ 3. _______________

Today I have touched: e.g. a pencil

1. _______________ 2. _______________ 3. _______________

Today I have smelt: e.g. perfume

1. ______________ 2. ______________ 3. ______________

Today I have tasted: e.g. cereal

1. ______________ 2. ______________ 3. ______________

2. Describing Images, Sounds, Objects, Smells and Tastes

Our life experiences provide us with pleasurable (positive) and painful (negative) memories which are useful for writing purposes. These life experiences are perceived through our five senses and give rise to feelings and reactions.

Description usually involves using adjectives. These are words that are linked with nouns and give more information.

For example, *A glorious day*. The adjective is 'glorious' and explains what kind of day it is.

Examples: Experiences perceived through the five senses.

Sight - An image - *A stunning landscape.*
Hearing - A sound - *The cooing of a dove.*
Touch - An object - *The soft fibres of a carpet.*
Smell - An aroma - *The strong smell of deodorant.*
Taste - A flavour - *The savoury taste of cheese.*

Exercise 1: 3 Write your own descriptions for each of the following:

Two Images: 1. ______________________________

2. ______________________________

Two Sounds: 1. Music
2. cars

Two Objects: 1. carpet
2. towel

Two Aromas: 1. deodorant
2. gosh

Two Flavours: 1. chocolate
2. ~~cheese~~ cheese

3. The Sixth Sense (Feelings)

Everybody has **Feelings** but they cannot be seen. They can only be shown by the way people behave.

If the characters in stories experience feelings, the readers of those stories can experience them too.

Information absorbed by the five senses gives rise to various feelings within people.

These feelings are often called intuition or the **Sixth Sense**.

Example: What feelings do we all experience?

Our feelings can include:

irritation; amusement; lethargy; apprehension; empathy; pensiveness; enthusiasm; being aggrieved; sadness.

Extreme feelings can include:

fury; horror; hopelessness; euphoria; elation.

Exercise 1: 4 List nine more feelings we all experience during our lives.

1. ______________ 2. ______________ 3. ______________
4. ______________ 5. ______________ 6. ______________
7. ______________ 8. ______________ 9. ______________

It is important to make characters in stories continually react to each other. These feelings can only be expressed when the characters take action in relation to other characters.

Example: In what ways do characters show their feelings?

Characters in stories might demonstrate their feelings by: *crying; staring; chuckling; backing away; kicking something; shaking; sweating; blushing; looking away; biting their nails; holding their nose; drumming their fingers;* etc.

Exercise 1: 5 Think of ten more things a character might do to show their feelings.

1. ______________ 6. ______________
2. ______________ 7. ______________
3. ______________ 8. ______________
4. ______________ 9. ______________
5. ______________ 10. ______________

4. Brainstorming Ideas

One approach is to **Brainstorm**, or list any ideas, once a story title or a particular character is decided upon.

Example: Write any words, phrases or sentences that come into mind with the title ***Betrayal***.

We might use the following words, phrases or sentences:
Words - *bitter; friend; smashed; attic; sprayed*
Phrases - *pouring rain; broken doll; rotten sandwich*
Sentences - *He twisted his ankle.; She scratched her face.*

Exercise 1: 6

Write any words, phrases or sentences using one of the following titles.

Choose from these titles: ***The Ghost***, ***The Letter***, ***The Catastrophe***, ***The Stranger***, ***The Dream*** or ***The Party***.

Use one of these characters: a **general**, a **witch**, a **nurse**, a **policeman**, a **vet**, a **plumber** or a **taxi driver**.

Five Words:

1. ________________ 2. ________________ 3. ________________

4. ________________ 5. ________________

Three Phrases:

1. ________________ 2. ________________ 3. ________________

Two Sentences:

1. ____

2. ____

Spider Diagrams or **Brain Maps** can help you brainstorm your thoughts and ideas and organise them on paper.

Example: Create a spider diagram or brain map for the story title ***The Deadly Fairground***.

We could use the six senses and write words and phrases.

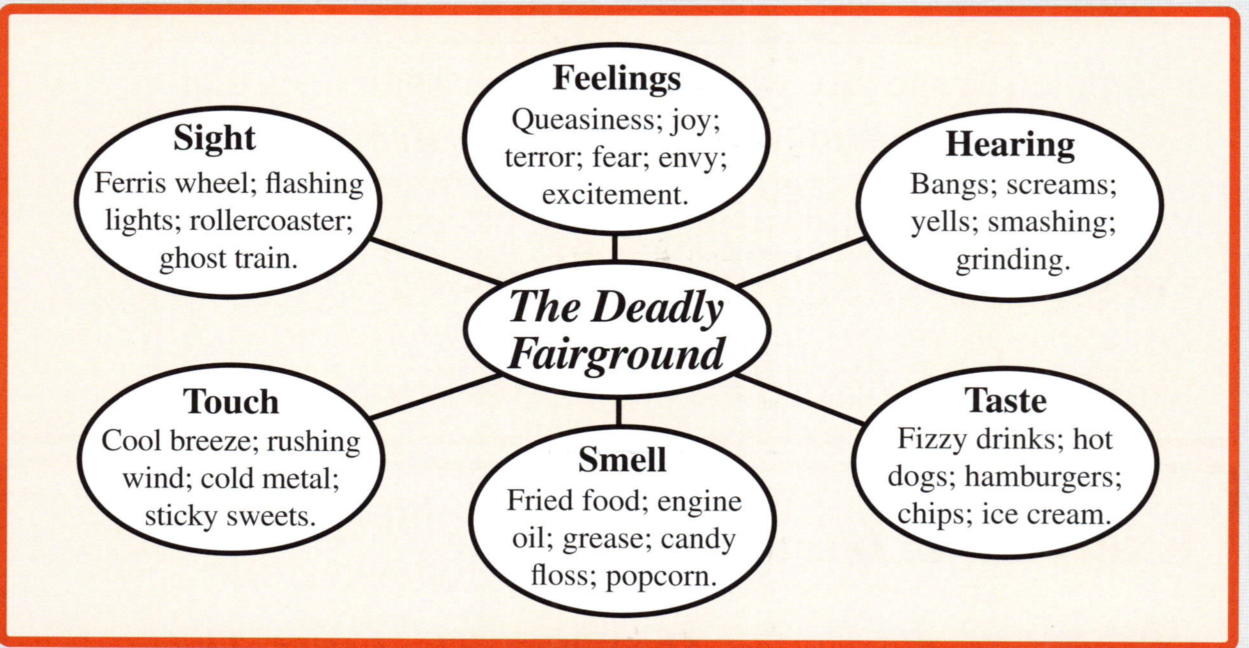

Spider diagrams or mind maps can be used to stimulate story ideas. They can have various categories. For example, the **Five Elements of Story** are:

Where • When • Who • What • Why

Another possibility is to use story subject areas:

Theme • Storyline • Event • Character • Issue • Memory

Exercise 1: 7

Add words or phrases to this spider diagram for the story title ***Lost City***:

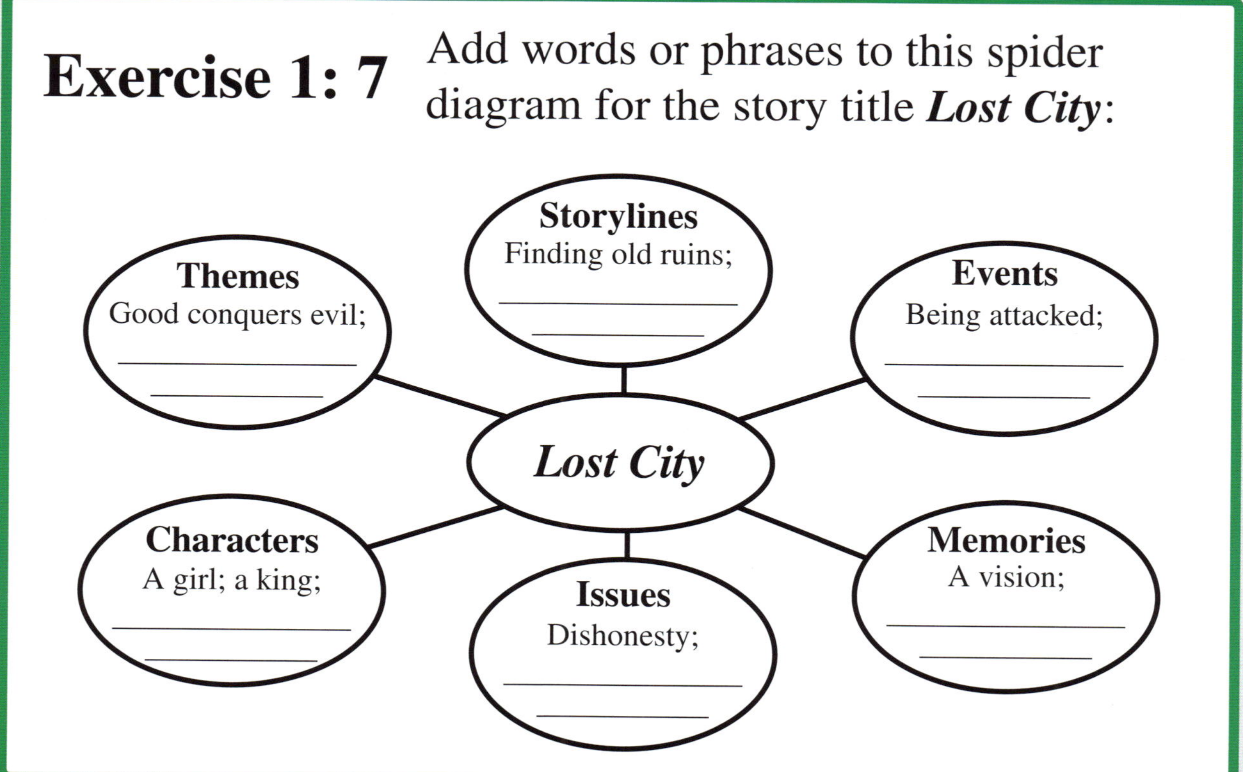

5. 'Stream of Consciousness'

This involves writing any ideas or thoughts that come into the mind at speed without editing them. Many useless things might be written, but amongst these words there may be ideas that can be used. A **'Stream of Consciousness'** can begin with any word, phrase or sentence.

Example: Write a 'stream of consciousness' for a story entitled ***A Nightmare***.

This is a 'stream of consciousness' for ***A Nightmare***. No editing has taken place.

There is a long dark tunnel stretching out before me. I run as fast as I can, but someone or something is closing in on me. It's really frightening and I don't think I can escape. There is a large crash just behind me. Rocks are falling from the roof of the tunnel and one has just missed me. I'm out of breath and I'm not sure how much further I can run. I feel the tunnel floor slope downwards, but there is only blackness ahead of me. Still, the pounding echo of steps draws nearer. Is there any way out? I stop and turn to face my pursuer. There is nothing else I can do.

Exercise 1: 8

Choose one of these titles and write a 'stream of consciousness': ***The Goal***, ***The Castle***, ***Runaway Train*** or ***The Jungle***.

____

____

____

____

6. Writing in Role

This is a development of the 'stream of consciousness' idea. A particular character is imagined and their thoughts and feelings are written down.

If it is written in the present tense it has more immediacy and feels as if it is happening right at that moment.

Again, it is important not to edit thoughts, but just to write. Whatever material is written can be edited later.

Example: Imagine you are a boy chimney sweep called Johnny in the Victorian era.

A boy like this would probably be illiterate, but this is just an exercise in using imagination to explore the character. We have to imagine he can write.

Remember it is written in present tense, e.g. *I feel* rather than *I felt*. Past tense is only used when Johnny recalls the past.

Writing in Role might produce something like this:

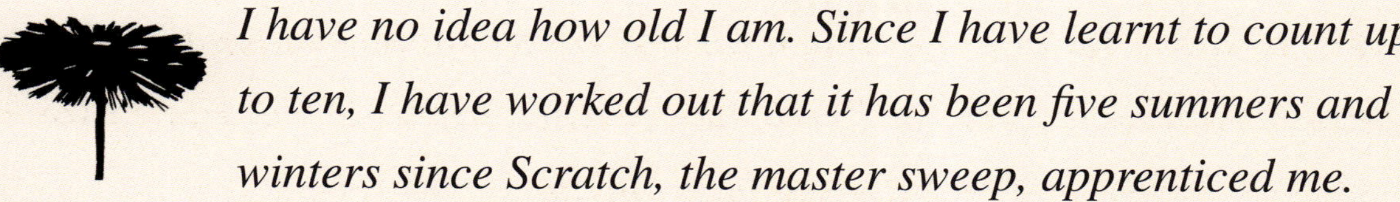

I have no idea how old I am. Since I have learnt to count up to ten, I have worked out that it has been five summers and winters since Scratch, the master sweep, apprenticed me. He was nicknamed Scratch because that's just what he does; scratch himself all over. It is now the sixth winter and the local parish has made me over to Scratch fully, and he owns me. For good measure, the parish

threw in Toby, my little brother, too. Scratch says he will be a burden until he is old enough to sweep - just another mouth to feed. Not that there is ever enough food anyway.

I can just about remember my mother before she died of typhus. Then, I was about the same size as Toby. I also recall when Toby was very small, so maybe I am older than ten. When I look into the cracked, dirty mirror by the door of the hovel, I can see my tattered overcoat no longer fits. My forearms now protrude from out of my woollen garment and my cotton trousers are too short. My shirt is ripped and there are only two buttons left. These are the only clothes I own, and I only ever take them off to wash them, which is rare.

Today, we are going to sweep in a big house in one of the London squares. I have collected all our brushes and they are in a large bundle by the doorway and Scratch told me that I'll be carrying them all. It's freezing cold outside and my feet are already turning blue.

I tug at Scratch's arm and venture: "Is there a piece of bread and a mug of tea today?"

Scratch ignores me, finishes the mouthful of bread he is eating and slurps some tea from a dirty old mug.

Toby cowers in the corner while Trixie, Scratch's wife, busies herself over the stove. He dare not reach for any of the spare food on the table. We only eat once a day, but Trixie and Scratch are well-fed. Her fulsome body and ruddy cheeks show she has a healthy appetite.

Scratch shoves me toward the doorway and yells, "Come on! It's time to go!"

Exercise 1: 9

Try one of these ideas for writing in role as a character (write as if you are the person in present tense):

- a girl or boy who falls down a manhole
- a paramedic who is first on the scene of a train crash
- a security guard who sees someone shoplifting

7. Special Memories

This is a very useful way to start a story. Everybody has **Special Memories** of places or events. These things stay in the mind in a very vivid way. This means descriptions are likely to be full of detail and can be an inspiration to write.

Example: Think of one special event and one special location that stands out in your memory.

Here is an example of the kind of memories of events and locations that might be fixed in a person's mind.

An event - Going on a special school trip.

A location - An impressive view of the mountains.

Exercise 1: 10 Think of and write down an event and a location that is special to you and remains very strong in your memory.

An event: ______________________________

A location: ______________________________

Example: Describe either the special event or the location in as much detail as possible.

This is any experience that occurred whilst visiting the Swiss Alps.

The North Face of the Eiger

As I looked out from the Eigerwand railway station viewing gallery that lies nearly 3,000 metres above sea level, the north face of the Eiger was only yards away. It was a remarkable feat of engineering to build a funicular railway in stages up to the highest point of the Swiss Alps.

From this vantage point it was possible to look out on a sheer wall of ice that was almost vertical.

The sunlight glistened on the blue ice that had glued itself to the rocks. Even from my position at the end of the access tunnel the air was crisp and pure. The only thing that separated me from one of the most dangerous and notorious climbs in the world, the Hinterstoisser Traverse, was a thick pane of glass. 'Eiger', commonly known as 'the Ogre', is an appropriate name for this treacherous mountain. The north face is a plumb line of ice and brittle limestone rock with large cracks and the tiniest of ledges. It is truly spectacular and it isn't hard to imagine being on 'death wall', as it is commonly called, pitched against the battering winds and extreme cold.

Then I saw them; up close to the glass were the latest party of three climbers, their harnesses roped together, inching their way up the sheer face. They hacked with ice picks at each staging point to fix more hooks in the rock for their pulleys and ropes. Then they hauled themselves up out of view. For a few lingering moments, I looked beyond the climbers and marvelled at the mountain peaks of the Swiss Jungfrau peninsula which dominates the horizon beyond the Eiger. The staggering beauty of this ancient glaciated region made me feel minute in comparison.

Exercise 1: 11 Describe either a special location or an event that is strong in your memory.

8. Characters from People you Know

Familiar people can form the basis for characters in stories.

Most authors have based their most interesting characters on people that they have come across or known very well.

Sometimes a character can be composed of a combination of traits from a number of people. It is crucial never to use the real names of people that are the basis for characters.

There are interesting people everywhere - **just observe**!

Example: Think of one interesting person you have known and describe them in a situation you remember.

The Granny I Never Had

It was a very sad day. All the family were there listening to the oration, but there was one extra person – me! I was attending the funeral of Mrs Evans, someone I had affectionately come to know as the grandmother I never really had. Most people can remember the doting care of a grandparent or even more than one. I can only remember seeing one of my grandmothers twice and, on both occasions, she was very ill, and being with one of my grandfathers once, when I sat on his knee as a small boy. As I listened to the warm words of the church minister, my mind reflected on the person I once knew as Mrs Evans.

She had been my landlady while I was at college. From the first day I met Mrs Evans, she decided I was special, just like all the other young men who had boarded at her house. Their photographs were proudly placed on the mantelpiece and my graduation photograph was soon added to the collection. However, I was the last of her boarders and we developed a closer relationship. She was small, slightly stooped, but sprightly and energetic. She announced proudly that she was 88 years old; exactly the same age as the Queen Mother who had been born in 1900. Astonishingly, her two daughters who lived close by could hardly keep up with her. Excellent meals that were fit for a king were prepared lovingly and cooked every day and conversation was lively. I think she was lonely, although there was no want of company, as she had a wonderful family. However, there had never been a son or a grandson. We were a perfect match; I had no grandmother and she had no grandson – we had found each other.

Mrs Evans was a wealth of historical information and vivid memories. She would speak of the Second World War and how a large bomb had destroyed many houses in the street, killed a number of residents and barely missed her house, the same one we were sitting in. Although her memories were freely shared, great sadness would always cloud her expression when she spoke of her late husband, as they had been devoted to each other. She often talked of him and how they had been married in a church near Chislehurst in Kent, but she had never been back there since the wedding.

One day I decided that I would take her there as a special treat. I watched her walk down the aisle of the church and recall those special events that had occurred nearly 70 years before. She sat in one of the pews for a number of minutes overcome with emotion and, with great dignity, thanked me from the bottom of her heart as we left. When I moved out and into my own home for the first time, Mrs Evans was one of the first visitors, no doubt to check its suitability and to check that I could look after myself.

We kept in touch for years after this. I frequently went back to her house for meals and a chat. There were visits to the hospital when she broke her hip and lost her mobility. There were phone calls to check how she was getting along. Then, there was her sudden and unexpected passing and the fact that I had had no chance to say goodbye.

As I stood there gazing at the small coffin that held the beloved Mrs Evans, I felt thankful to have known her and whispered affectionately, "Goodbye, Grandma!"

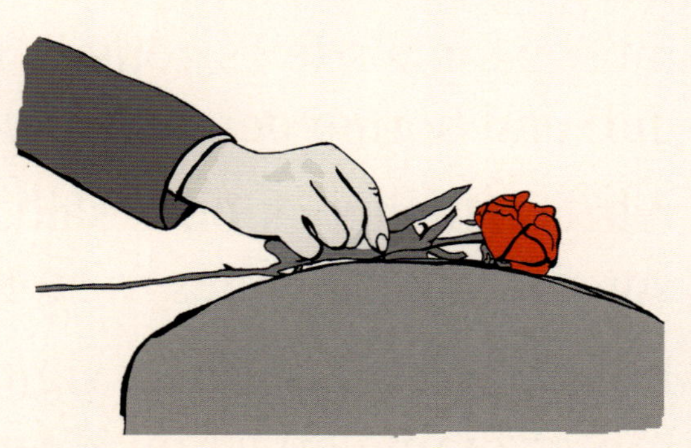

Exercise 1: 12 Think of a memory about an interesting character you know and write about it.

9. Dramatic Life Events

Biographical material is sometimes interesting. However, most people's lives contain some interesting events and many dull and boring details which are of no interest to a reader.

Alfred Hitchcock once said, 'Drama is life with the dull bits cut out'. This applies to story writing just as much.

It is important to select significant events that have had some life-changing effect on a person for it to be interesting.

Example: Write about an interesting life event that had a real impact on the way you think and behave now.

This event occurred on my way home from work one day.

The Car Crash

A crash is something that we know can happen if we drive a car, but we usually push it to the back our minds. Driving a car is dangerous, as it involves hurtling around at high speeds in a metal box and, if something goes wrong or someone makes a mistake, it can have devastating consequences.

I remember returning along a familiar route after a day's work. The weather was good and the spring sun warmed the inside of the new car I had recently purchased. All I was thinking about was getting home and the rest of the tasks I had to accomplish that day. Then it happened. I drove across a roundabout as the road was clear and I had right of way. The national speed limit was 60mph on that particular road and the roundabout had four exits. I slowed, but was still travelling at considerable speed and was not expecting to have to stop quickly.

All of a sudden, a red Ford Fiesta pulled across my path. For a moment time seemed to stand still and I knew I was going to crash into the car. I felt terrified, as I careered towards the other car. I stepped on the brakes and the car began to skid, as I flung the steering wheel to the right in an attempt to lessen the impact. It was like a film in slow motion. The car swerved and I remember having the terrible feeling of being unable to control what would happen next. The impact was sudden and devastating; a loud crash and a thud as my car ploughed into the side of the red car. It resulted in a tangled concertina of metal and an explosion of glass, as it shattered and burst. Both cars were misshapen by the shock. It was like a joust and someone had to come off worse. My car had hit the driver's side of the other car which was stove in like a vee. The offside wing of my car was badly damaged. Then silence – both cars were still. I sat shaking and felt numb for a few seconds. I had survived unhurt.

My mind then turned to the occupants of the other car. Immediately, I thought I was to blame. Were they hurt? I eased open the door of my battered car and rushed over to the red Ford. The door was badly damaged and crumpled inwards. A middle-aged man and woman sat staring ahead. The woman was the driver and she seemed uninjured.

I ventured, "Are you all right?"

I was desperate to know they weren't hurt. In those moments, I assumed the accident was my fault, as I had hit her car. Her head slowly turned in my direction and she directed her gaze at me.

In a hostile tone, she barked, "You were going too fast and drove into me."

I was stunned, as my only concern a few moments before had been their welfare. However, her comments shook me, and I quickly reflected on the situation.

"Wait a minute," I said, "you pulled across my path. I had right of way. Here am I, only concerned for your welfare and I'm blamed for an accident you caused. I don't care about my car or yours. The fact is we're all safe and that's what matters."

I reflected; how often people who are in the wrong try to shift the blame onto others. I had been willing to take responsibility for the accident had it been my fault. The police soon arrived and took statements and it was clear to them from the position of the cars that I was not to blame. This was confirmed by my insurance company, and their insurance company was forced to pay out for the damage to both cars.

The accident left me feeling vulnerable in a car. I learnt that the careless actions of others or ourselves can destroy life in a moment. I think it has made me drive more cautiously ever since, and to be constantly aware of the potential mistakes others can make in just a split second. I now try to anticipate the actions of other road users, whilst being aware that I, too, am an imperfect driver and must always take the greatest care.

Exercise 1: 13 Think of an interesting event you or someone you know has experienced and write about it here.

10. Literature and other Sources

Ideas for writing can come from many different **Sources**.

Inspiration can come from images and words from the arts and visual media such as film, television, photographs, paintings, dance, sculpture, theatre and museums.

Other literary forms such as poetry, plays, novels, historical material, short stories and articles can also provide ideas.

Literature is always a good source. Studying successful writers can inspire great ideas for character and storyline.

Example: Demonstrate how ideas can come from a great novel like ***Nicholas Nickleby*** by Charles Dickens.

In this extract Nicholas Nickleby, a teaching assistant, confronts the cruel schoolmaster Wackford Squeers for his mistreatment of his pupils at Dotheboys Hall.

Smike, a poor, pathetic drudge and servant who was continually ill, looked pitiful.

"Have you anything to say, Smike?" demanded Squeers again: giving his right arm two or three flourishes to try the cane's power and suppleness. "Stand a little out of the way, Mrs Squeers, my dear; I've hardly got room enough."

"Spare me, sir!" cried Smike.

"Oh! that's all, is it?" said Squeers. "Yes, I'll flog you within an inch of your life, and spare you that."

"Ha, ha, ha," laughed Mrs Squeers, "that's a good 'un!"

"A nasty, ungrateful, pig-headed, brutish, obstinate, sneaking dog," exclaimed Mrs Squeers, taking Smike's head under her arm.

"Stand aside, my dear," replied Squeers.

Mrs Squeers, being out of breath with her exertions, complied. Squeers caught the boy firmly in his grip; one desperate blow of the cane had fallen on his body — he was wincing from the lash and uttering a scream of pain — it was raised again, and again about to fall — when Nicholas Nickleby, suddenly starting up, cried "Stop!" in a voice that made the rafters ring.

"Who cried stop?" said Squeers, turning savagely round.

"I," said Nicholas, stepping forward. "This must not go on."

"Must not go on!" cried Squeers, almost in a shriek.

"No!" thundered Nicholas.

Aghast and stupefied by the boldness of the interference, Squeers released his hold of Smike, and, falling back a pace or two, gazed upon Nicholas with looks that were positively frightful.

"I say must not," repeated Nicholas, nothing daunted; "shall not. I will prevent it."

Squeers continued to gaze upon him, with his eyes starting out of his head; but he was so astonished he was momentarily bereft of speech.

"Sit down, beggar!" screamed Squeers, almost beside himself with rage, and seizing Smike as he spoke.

"Wretch," rejoined Nicholas, fiercely, "touch him at your peril! I will not stand by. My blood is up!"

"Stand back," cried Squeers, brandishing his weapon.

"I have many insults to avenge," said Nicholas, flushed with passion; "and I am enraged at the cruel treatment of these helpless little mites in this foul excuse for a school."

Nicholas had scarcely spoken, when Squeers, in a violent outbreak of wrath, and with a cry like the howl of a wild beast, spat upon him, and struck him a blow across the face with the cane. Smarting with the agony of the blow, Nicholas sprang upon him, seized the weapon from his hand, pinned him by the throat and beat the ruffian until he begged for mercy.

An extract from *Nicholas Nickleby* by Charles Dickens (1812-1870).

Ideas about Characters and Storyline

Details about Smike could provide ideas for characters.

This extract is about the ill-treatment of children and could provide ideas for a story about any young person who suffers cruelty.

Smike is an **orphan** and has no living relatives. He works as a servant at Dotheboys Hall. He is ill-treated and suffers continual beatings.

The **schoolmaster** is well-fed, self-satisfied and cruel.

The **storyline** of Nicholas Nickleby includes the life story and eventual sad fate of Smike.

Many children's stories tell the story of a child who has experienced great difficulties or childhood trauma.

Exercise 1: 14

Think of a story you have read or a film you have seen. Make notes about the main characters and the storyline that could inspire your own story.

____

____

____

____

____

____

____

____

____

Your Own Story - Draft One

Now write your own story using one of the following scenarios. There are two story scenarios to choose from:

Story 1 - *The Tree House* or **Story 2 - *Locked In***

Write Story 1 or 2 in this book. Once you have learnt the principles, you can write the other story.

Try and include ideas and techniques from Chapter One.

Chapter 1 - Story Starting Points

Inspiration for writing stories can occur in many ways. Some forms of stimulus work better for one person and others work better for another. It is important to choose the ones below that work for best you.

1. ***The Five Senses*** - sight, hearing, touch, smell and taste
2. ***Images, Sounds, Objects, Smells & Tastes*** - experiences
3. ***The Sixth Sense*** - feelings
4. ***Brainstorming Ideas*** - using lists and spider diagrams
5. ***'Stream of Consciousness'*** - writing without editing
6. ***Writing in Role*** - in present tense as the character
7. ***Special Memories*** - locations or events
8. ***Characters from People you Know*** - people you have met
9. ***Dramatic Life Events*** - your life experiences
10. ***Literature and other Sources*** - things you have read

Observe these Rules and complete the Story

1. The character is not allowed to leave the space. Find a way to end the story in the space without leaving it.
2. One other character can enter the space and leave it at some point in the story.
3. Write out the scenario first and then continue the story.

First Draft - Story 1

The Tree House

Opening Scenario in Past Tense:

I had climbed the ladder to the tree house some hours before and pulled it up behind me. Now I was safe - well for now anyway. I had built the tree house the previous summer and now it was my only place of refuge. It had been a terrifying day. But now nobody knew where I was; at least I hoped so. There were a few meagre supplies of food I had stored in the corner. I looked out of the small opening that served as a window and wondered what would happen next...

First Draft - Story 2

Locked In

Opening Scenario in Past Tense:

I tried the front door in the flat but it was locked. Then I went to the windows but they were all sealed. I took out a penknife and dug away at the seals until they gave way. I looked out, but I was four storeys up. The new landlord had put bars on the opening to stop anybody desperate enough to jump. Who had locked me in and why? I went back to the door and thumped on it as hard as I could. Silence. There was a telephone on the coffee table. I picked up the receiver. It was dead. I had no mobile phone or any other of my belongings with me. What was I going to do?

Choose to write either **Story 1** or **Story 2**, then use the Planning page to write down some ideas for your story.

Planning - 1st Draft

Story 1 - *The Tree House*

or Story 2 - *Locked In*

Now let's write a story.

Choose either ***The Tree House*** or ***Locked In*** and copy out the opening scenario on Story Page 1 - 1st Draft, then continue your story on the pages that follow.

Story Page 1 - 1st Draft

The Tree House or ***Locked In***

Shock

Story Page 2 - 1st Draft

The Tree House or ***Locked In***

Intrigue

Story Page 3 - 1st Draft

The Tree House or ***Locked In***

Concern

Story Page 4 - 1st Draft

The Tree House* or *Locked In

Fright

Story Page 5 - 1st Draft

The Tree House or ***Locked In***

Panic

Story Page 6 - 1st Draft

The Tree House or ***Locked In***

Terror

Scores Out of Ten	Spelling & Grammar →		Creativity →	

Chapter 2
Texture & Dynamics

Texture refers to how important components of the story are woven together like a garment to create interest for the reader.

Dynamics refer to the levels of emotion or excitement generated in the reader by the story content. The level of intensity can rise and fall like the volume in a piece of music.

1. Texture

Story Texture has four components:

Mood • Atmosphere
Intrigue or Curiosity • Surprise

a. Mood

Mood refers to the particular state of mind of one of the central characters. The way that character feels will then dominate the whole storyline. If the main character is sad then this mood is communicated to the reader or audience.

Example: Write a story called ***The History of Johnny Sweep*** which demonstrates the main character's mood as one of panic.

Johnny panics inside the chimney and this sense of panic dominates the storyline.

Johnny scrambled into the tightest space. It measured no more than a foot across and 18 inches the other way. His knees were virtually touching his chin. He could

hardly breathe for the choking fumes and swirling black soot that arose from below. Coughing was no use, as it left him gasping for air and he knew he would suck in even more coal dust. He was accustomed to fear – he hated the small cramped corners, and the twists and turns of the chimney. He held the brush tightly, as one slip would send it sliding back down the shaft, and he knew what that would mean. A beating would await him and he would be sent straight back up the dirty hole above the fireplace. Johnny would have to climb again and he was tired and exhausted. It was early in the morning, although he had no idea of the real time. He saw clocks on walls but he had never learnt how to read them. What did it matter anyhow? Much of his life was spent in the pitch-black darkness of a chimney.

He had to reach the blockage, but how far up the chimney was it? He had already climbed and shimmied up about 20 feet. He used his knees, which were rammed up the other side of the chimney, to hold himself in place, while he stretched for each handhold. He had reached the next bend in the chimney. The last semblance of light from below would be extinguished immediately he pulled himself up into the diagonal shaft that angled off the main chimney.

Heat came up from below. He knew Scratch had become impatient and had lit the fire in the grate. Urgency was now required. He would either suffocate if he stayed in the flue or burn to death if he fell. But where was the blockage? He had to find it, but time was against him. Scratch had no concern for his safety. Johnny felt desperate.

Now think of ***The Tree House*** or ***Locked In***. There is an opportunity for the character to show any number of moods that might dominate the storyline.

The character might panic initially when he or she realises that escaping or leaving the room or space will be very difficult. This might give way to a mood of depression when he or she feels like giving up.

The main character might exude fear if the other character who enters the room acts in a threatening or suspicious manner. Fear might grow into terror if a direct threat is made against the main character.

Exercise 2: 1

Think about ***The Tree House*** or ***Locked In***. Give your main character a mood that will pervade part of the story. Write notes or extracts for the next draft.

b. Atmosphere

Atmosphere in scientific terms refers to the gaseous environment (oxygen, carbon dioxide, etc.) that makes life possible on Earth. In a story, atmosphere refers to the general tone or feeling that has been created by the writer, but it does not necessarily come specifically from the characters.

Example: Create a dreamy, nostalgic and sentimental atmosphere in a story entitled ***Florence Bovington Goes East***.

This story is about a wealthy young girl who lives in the most select part of Victorian London.

Florence loved the crisp morning mist that rose over Tillotson Square in which she lived. She often got up early to watch the sun rise over the distant chimneys and rooftops of the great city of London. The sunlight reflected on the white walled buildings that enclosed the square and everything looked bright and airy. A few workers tramped through the square, but it was mostly empty. There was a fenced off communal garden in the centre of the square that could be accessed only by the occupants of the houses. This garden was furnished with water features, footpaths and flowerbeds. On rare occasions Florence was allowed into the garden for her daily walk, and this is something she relished. There were bright red roses and daffodils, and Florence loved to see them sway in the breeze, the bees buzz from flower to flower, and the butterflies flutter through the air.

Florence was rarely allowed out of the three-storey town house unless she was escorted by Rose, one of the trusted young servants, or her austere governess, Mrs Stevens. The holidays were particularly trying, as Florence only had friends at her exclusive boarding school and felt extremely lonely when she came home. Her mother, Lady Bovington, was always busy chairing important meetings of the Women's Institute as part of her charity work, or accompanying her husband, the Right Honourable Nigel Bovington, member of parliament for one of the most respectable parliamentary seats in the House of Commons. Florence could never remember which one, but she knew it was one of the most important.

As she gazed out of her bedroom window on this particular morning, it was very dull. Drizzle spattered against the window pane and Florence felt a pang of emptiness inside her that matched the miserable weather. There was no one to talk to. Breakfast would be served at eight o'clock in the parlour and she would eat it alone, as Mother would be leaving early.

Florence turned back to her dressing table to comb out her long ringlets. She had just turned 13 years old, but she still didn't feel pretty. As she sat at the dresser, she wondered if other children felt like her. Her blue eyes sparkled and filled with tears. She would read her book today, go for her customary walk with Rose and then wait for her mother to return. Then some of her mother's charity committee would arrive and there would be tea and scones in the drawing room. Florence would be required to make an appearance and endure the formal introductions before being ushered from the room. Florence sighed and adjusted the large pink bow at the front of her white lace dress.

Think about ***The Tree House*** or ***Locked In***.

If the treehouse is a long way from the ground and the ladder has been withdrawn, this would make the situation more frightening.

If an atmosphere is created where there are echoing footsteps, bars on the windows, an iron bedstead and a peephole in the door, it would seem like the character is in a locked cell.

Exercise 2: 2 Make notes or write an extract creating atmosphere in ***The Tree House*** or ***Locked In***.

____

____

____

____

____

____

____

____

____

____

c. Intrigue or Curiosity

Intrigue or **Curiosity** is created in a story when something mysterious or strange happens. Human beings are naturally curious and inquisitive and will want to solve a mystery.

For example, interest and fascination is created immediately by using magical and incredible elements in a story.

Example: Using ***Florence Bovington Goes East***, generate a feeling of intrigue or curiosity in the reader.

Florence waits for a Hansom Cab with her mother at the corner of Tillotson Square. Florence becomes fascinated with a working class girl who is also waiting for someone with her mother.

Just as they reached the corner of the square, a couple of middle-class status was boarding a hansom cab. To the irritation of Lady Bovington, they did not stand aside; even though the cab driver dismounted from his seat above the rear of the carriage and climbed down to indicate they should. Lady Bovington looked away to signify her disapproval and fixed her gaze on the gardens. She then held this position as the cab prepared to pull away, to show those who should know better that her figure in profile was still of a higher standing than them; even if they could travel in the cab and she was stationary. Florence found all this social manoeuvring rather tiresome. She thought it simply better to ask the couple for the cab, because they might be late for the theatre. However, Lady Bovington saw the idea of actually conversing with members of the public, and requesting something from them, as an intolerable breach of etiquette. After all, they might say no; and then where would she be?

They had to wait. Florence watched the horse rear up in response to the driver's whip and the cab sped away. She stood alongside her mother and Rose positioned herself at a suitable distance. There was no conversation. Florence only ever had formal exchanges with her mother and they had grown apart. Displays of emotion were discouraged, so if Florence was upset she would cry alone. She rarely spent time with her mother, so even polite conversation was strained. Now she found herself standing awkwardly on the street corner with her, and she felt more uncomfortable than ever. Their statuesque-like pose seemed unnatural to those on the street around them. However, Florence had no choice but to behave in the same way no matter how self-conscious it made her feel.

Florence gradually became aware of two more people standing nearby, right on corner of the street. The first was a girl of about her own age. She was dressed in a smock and wearing an apron. Unlike Florence, who felt constrained by the strictures of her mother, this girl seemed completely unselfconscious. She pulled at her hair under her bonnet, swayed from side to side, and kicked the heels of her worn out shoes into the paving because she seemed to enjoy the noise it made. Florence noticed she was rather unkempt and scruffy. Her apron was smudged and the sleeves of her blouse were threadbare. However, she appeared to care nothing about how she looked or dressed. The woman next to her seemed to be her mother. Her attire was similar, although her clothing was somewhat shabbier. Every now and then, the woman said something to the girl, and Florence observed she had no front teeth.

Why were they standing there, just a few yards from one of the wealthiest squares in London? These were poor people and Florence had rarely ever seen them up close.

Exercise 2: 3

Think of an intriguing or mysterious event that could happen in ***The Tree House*** or ***Locked In*** and write some notes or extracts here.

d. Surprise

Surprise is a useful story device. This is when something totally unexpected happens in a story. Human beings love surprises because they are out of the ordinary.

It can involve the main character finding or discovering something. Perhaps the character is subjected to kidnapping or assault without warning. Maybe they could be presented with an unusual gift or find themselves in a strange situation.

Example: Using ***The History of Johnny Sweep***, create a big surprise by building a totally unexpected event into the story.

Johnny and Toby are accustomed to cruel and unpleasant treatment, but they are taken by surprise in one house.

Out they went into the street. After a bracing walk in the cold morning air through the old streets of the city, they eventually arrived at the square in Belgravia. The party entered a large Georgian house via the tradesman's entrance at the rear. The maid showed them into a large reception room. It was filled with expensive furniture, and vases full of flowers graced every flat surface. The room had a large grate.

This was their first appointment in this spacious and sumptuous residence. Mrs Blackstone awaited them. She was attired in a silk dress and a stylish bonnet. Johnny and Toby had never seen anyone like her before. Her blue eyes blinked with concern, as she gazed down at the pitiful specimen that was Toby. He coughed and could barely stand.

"Wait here," she said, and hurried out.

Johnny looked around the parlour. It was full of polished furniture and beautiful paintings. A large potted Christmas tree stood in the corner ready to be decorated. He noticed a picture frame on a dresser. It contained what he thought was a photograph. Johnny had never seen one of these sepia images before. It was of a small boy, dressed in fine clothes and a cap.

She soon returned alongside a maid, who carried two large glasses of milk on a silver tray. Mrs Blackstone noticed Johnny gazing at the picture.

"That was Sebastian, my son." Her expression looked sad.

Scratch shuffled impatiently as she offered first Toby and then Johnny a glass. They devoured the delicious substance in a few gulps.

"There!" Mrs Blackstone announced. "And when you've finished, Mr Scratch, these boys are to come in here again for some bread and cheese before they go."

Mrs Blackstone was a woman of her word, and the boys ate bread and cheese to their hearts' delight once the sweep was completed, while Scratch waited in an embarrassed and furious temper.

Once the boys had finished, Mrs Blackstone addressed Scratch.

"Mr Scratch, don't you feed your charges?"

He reddened, "'Eartily ma'am. They're nearly eatin' me and me wife out of 'ouse and 'ome."

Exercise 2: 4 Think of a surprising or unexpected event that could happen in ***The Tree House*** or ***Locked In*** and write extracts or notes on it here.

2. Dynamics

Dynamics has four components:

Tension • **Suspense** • **Anticipation** • **Conflict**

a. Tension

Tension in a story can be compared to a 'slow burn candle'. Events must keep occurring in the story to hold the interest of the reader. These can be understood as either **complications** in the plot (storyline) or **problems** the main character has to face and solve.

Throughout the story the pressure must be kept up and maintained otherwise engagement will be lost. However, the tension can vary in its level of intensity.

It is like watching a football match. It is a more exciting match to watch if the teams are continually putting each other under pressure and both sides seem as if they can win.

Example: Using ***The History of Johnny Sweep***, maintain the tension by building in problems that put the main character under pressure.

Toby is forced to make his first climb up a chimney by Scratch.

Johnny had completed his sweep of the main chimney. He had bagged up the valuable soot and taken it outside, ready to be collected later by another master sweep, with whom Scratch had made a deal, who sold the stuff. Scratch would let it go for 9 pence a bushel, more money than Johnny would ever see in a year.

It was now Toby's turn. They had been led to the humbler surroundings of the dining area of the servants' quarters. Scratch pushed Toby towards the hearth.

"Up yer go then, little'n. Jump to it!"

Toby stared up at the tiny flue from under the hearth, his feet covered with dust and prickling from the warm embers of the dying fire. It was

filthy and smelly. He looked up into the square hole just above him. It seemed just large enough but was no broader than a forearm's width across.

"You'll go up it, and there'll be no complainin', you 'ear? When yer get up there, yer brush it 'ard, understand, and scrape it if need be."

Toby hesitated.

"Up yer go, or you don't eat and I'll throw yer out."

Toby coughed profusely as the soot from the chimney sprayed him.

Johnny brushed him down and whispered, "Climb fast."

Scratch fed up the main sweeping pole and then tucked a small brush and a scraper into Toby's tiny hand. Toby began to sniffle.

Scratch pointed to the sweep pole, "So yer direct it at each turn as soon as yer gets past it."

Toby scrambled up and placed one foot onto the first ledge. Johnny saw his chest heave. He was already crying. Scratch clamped his other leg hard and pushed him up.

"Shut it. Go!"

It is important to make things happen in ***The Tree House*** or ***Locked In*** to maintain the level of tension.

For example, one other character might be involved; a meal might be delivered through a hatch; things could be found in the room or space (maybe some human remains); an escape attempt could be foiled; the tree might become unstable; a flashback or flashforward could be built into the story.

Exercise 2: 5 Write some extracts for your character in ***The Tree House*** or ***Locked In*** and maintain the tension by making unexpected things happen.

____

____

____

____

____

____

____

____

____

____

b. Suspense

Suspense can be compared to a 'quick burn firework'. Suspense occurs when tension is built up quickly and there is much more at stake for the characters.

It often involves a life threatening situation for the main character. Tension created through suspense is usually released quickly. Suspense is only effective if it is used sparingly in stories.

Example: Using ***The History of Johnny Sweep***, create suspense by building events to a climax.

As Toby climbs the chimney he gets stuck and the situation develops into a life-threatening crisis.

Toby disappeared and Johnny's heart sank. Would he ever see him again? Scratch covered up the hearth, to catch any soot, with the cloth that had served as a blanket for the boys each night. A pile of soot showered down every few minutes, but then it stopped.

Scratch and Johnny climbed up the servants' staircase to the loft space, and then out of a roof light and onto the roof. They waited by the smallest chimney: nothing. Johnny thought of Moriarty and his final climb. It didn't even look like Toby would survive his first. The agonising wait continued.

Johnny put his ear to the head of the chimney. He could hear some scuffling. Some thuds were followed by a whine – a sound Johnny knew.

"He's stuck!"

"Serves 'im right. Didn't do it right."

Johnny glared at Scratch.

"Won't get another job 'ere then."

Johnny's fists clenched. Scratch was near the edge and his impulse

was to push him off the roof. But instead, Johnny rushed back towards the roof light. Finishing off Scratch wasn't worth hanging for.

"'Ere, where you goin'?"

In a moment, Johnny was through the roof light and onto the stairwell. The butler, who was on his way up with morning tea for the master of the house, greeted him.

Johnny spluttered, "Is there another way into the chimney?"

"It hasn't been opened up for years."

Johnny fought back the tears.

"My brother's trapped."

"Wait!"

The butler gave the tray to a passing maid and led Johnny across a landing to another servant's passage. They descended one flight and there was a grating on the wall. The butler undid four clamps and tried to ease it back. Johnny joined in, and they both slid their fingers behind the iron grate and pulled. They felt it give way and lifted it off. Clouds of dirt and dust wafted into the stairwell.

Johnny stuck his head through the hole. Where was Toby? Was it too late?

Johnny listened then yelled, "Toby!"

In ***The Tree House*** or ***Locked In***, suspense can be built in a number of different ways. Perhaps the character who enters the room or space could threaten or endanger the main character and this causes uncertainty and fear.

Maybe the room or space begins to fill up with water or choking fumes or catches fire and the character cannot easily escape. The main character could risk their life even more to escape from the room or space if more things go wrong.

Exercise 2: 6 Make notes or write a short extract for ***The Tree House*** or ***Locked In*** that moves it from tension to suspense.

____

____

____

____

____

____

____

____

____

____

c. *Anticipation*

Anticipation is when there is a strong inkling of what might happen next. A high level of tension or suspense does not necessarily mean a reader will know exactly what is coming next, but it is often something life-threatening.

For example, if someone is swimming in the sea and sharks are encircling them, only the dorsal fins might be seen. However, that is enough for a reader to anticipate a scene of carnage and imagine the fear of being eaten.

Example: Using the story ***The Music Box***, create a situation where the reader can anticipate what might happen next.

Katrine plays the piano, but her aunt does not approve.

Behind the misty condensation on the glass, Katrine sits at a grand piano. The small, delicate fingers of one hand range over the keys and play the tune of a beautiful lullaby. She plays a glissando and then embellishes the music with great dexterity and skill.

The servants stand in a line before Aunt Eugene in the servants' dining room.

"I'll tolerate no careless work of any kind..."

Aunt Eugene falters and stares in the direction of the music. She glances around confused. Although perturbed, Aunt Eugene recovers her composure.

"No shoddy actions and..."

Aunt Eugene again fumbles for words. The servants shift about.

Katrine's eyes are now wet with tears and, as her sobs grow louder, she plays the melody even more passionately.

Aunt Eugene barks, "Dismissed, all of you. Go!"
The servants scurry off. Aunt Eugene heads for the library.

Through her tears Katrine strains to read the ledger lines from a dog-eared and scruffy old Mozart music score. The dulcet tones reverberate around a large, wood-panelled room with peeling wallpaper, hung with old portraits and with dusty book shelves that reach up to a cracked plaster ceiling. A single candle holder sits on the piano. As the light from the candle flickers across the faces of the ancestors staring out from the pictures, it almost seems as if they are listening to her playing.

Suddenly, a distant but rasping high-pitched voice is heard through the open door, "Katrine, don't run from me."

Katrine slams the lid of the piano. Outside the window, some snow breaks away from the ledge and falls to the ground. The robin flies off into what has now become a blizzard. Katrine grabs her music score, stomps out of the room and turns left into a long, wood-panelled corridor. It opens out into a large, marble hallway with a winding stone staircase.

Again, the angry voice yells, "Where are you Katrine? Come here immediately."

It echoes down the corridor behind her and into the grand marble hallway. Katrine quickly scampers up the stairway. As she enters a corridor that leads off the balcony, she hears the heavy thud of footsteps on the stone stairs.

Katrine rushes towards a door and enters. She closes it behind her with a sigh of relief. It is a spacious bedroom with oak floorboards and a ceiling stained by rainwater from a recent leak. On the left-hand side of the room is a large four-poster bed with a bedraggled brown teddy lying on it. To the right of the bed is a dresser and an open violin case lies on it. In front, by the window, sits a large toy box and, next to that, a rocking horse.

Katrine's face tenses as she hears the echo of quick footsteps outside, which suddenly stop.

A muffled angry voice sounds, "I've told you before."

Katrine steps away from the door as it swings open. A stout looking middle-aged woman enters. It is Aunt Eugene. The backdraught from the door makes the candle on the dresser gutter. The flickering light across the angry features of the woman gives them a devilish quality.

Katrine draws back towards the window and turns away. Aunt Eugene follows her in a flash, forcefully grabs her arm and pulls her round to face her. Katrine hangs her head to avoid the piercing gaze.

"You are not to play that piano."

Katrine hides the music behind her back.

She looks up with tears in her eyes, "I wish my father was still alive."

The woman draws herself up to her full height, "You ungrateful little wretch. How dare you! After all I've done for you. I took you in. Now, you'll stay in your room until I say you can come out. Do you understand?"

Exercise 2: 7 Think of an event that could happen in ***The Tree House*** or ***Locked In***. Write extracts or notes on this that build the level of anticipation up to the point the event occurs.

d. Conflict

For a story to work there must be **Conflict** right from the start. **Conflict between the characters is essential.** Always make the main characters want different things and then they will have disagreements. Even characters who are on the same side should have different perspectives and views.

There can also be conflict with nature, e.g. climbing a very dangerous mountain; dealing with a serious fire; the dangers of a shipwreck at sea; an earthquake or hurricane, etc.

Example: Using ***Florence Bovington Goes East***, indicate how the characters are in conflict with each other.

Florence is in conflict with her mother because she finds it hard to live up to her expectations.

Why were they standing there, just a few yards from one of the wealthiest squares in London? These were poor people and Florence had rarely ever seen them up close.

Suddenly, a middle-aged man appeared from the other side of the street and made straight for them. He was shoddily dressed and his complexion bronzed by the elements. As soon as he reached the mother and daughter, he took off his cap, held it out close to the girl, and shook it aggressively. Lady Bovington was completely oblivious to these occurrences, since her head was still turned away, whilst Florence was completely engrossed in the unfolding drama. The mother took the girl's hand and tried to guide her away, but the man was insistent and blocked their path.

"Give it 'ere," he slurred.

With a flick of the head, Lady Bovington assessed the situation and stepped a few more paces to her left. Florence dutifully followed but kept watching the scene.

The man was obviously drunk, and this appeared to make the woman start to weep. Florence was surprised by the sudden show of uncontrolled emotion and her interest was piqued.

"Tilly! 'And it over now!"

Florence whispered to herself, "Tilly."

The girl clung to her mother and looked around for support. Florence appeared to offer it with her sympathetic expression and the two girls locked eyes. The man lifted a fist and Tilly cowered.

Florence wanted to assist, but Lady Bovington sensed her fascination with the dispute and took another step sideways. Florence felt obliged to do her mother's bidding and followed suit.

"Florence, you must keep away from such people."

Now both Tilly and her mother were in floods of tears. Tilly finally held out her apron, reached in, pulled out a few pennies, and dropped them into the cap.

"All of it," the man snarled.

Tilly handed over the rest. The man staggered away.

Florence listened closely to the words that followed.

The mother remonstrated, "How can we eat now?"

Tilly hugged her mother. Florence was touched by the warmth and affection between them. Tilly seemed to notice Florence's interest and again their eyes met. Florence looked upon her with kindness, and although Tilly's eyes were red and swollen with tears, she was heartened by Florence's compassionate response and her face brightened.

Lady Bovington took a step forward.

"Here's our cab."

She hailed the arriving Hansom with a delicate wave of her umbrella and walked towards it. Florence hesitated, and then moved in the same direction. She wanted in some way to connect with Tilly, so she tugged out a lace handkerchief from her sleeve and let it fall as she passed her.

The girl scrambled for it in a rather undignified way and held it out to Florence.

"Miss, yer dropped it."

Lady Bovington had entered the cab by now and the driver kept the door open for Florence.

Florence took the handkerchief and smiled, "Thank you... Tilly."

"Yer know me name, miss?"

Florence whispered again, "I heard your mother say it. I hope you didn't mind me using it."

Tilly shook her head.

Lady Bovington tapped her umbrella with impatience against the panelling of the cab.

Florence whispered, "I take a walk with Rose, my maid, on Sundays at 4 o'clock in the garden over there. Meet me there."

Tilly was puzzled. Florence got into the cab and it drove off.

"Child, I hope you weren't consulting with that creature."

"No, Mama, she kindly returned my handkerchief and I thanked her."

This was the first lie Florence had ever told her mother. She felt a little guilty, but it also felt somewhat pleasurable, because she had been somewhat mischievous for the first time too.

In ***The Tree House*** or ***Locked In***, it is important to create conflict between the main character and the other character that enters the room or space. Threatening or suspicious behaviour can create a confrontation between the characters, particularly if a life-threatening situation happens.

Conflict can also occur through encounters with characters in flashback or flashforward situations.

Exercise 2: 8

Think about ***The Tree House*** or ***Locked In***. Create, rewrite or make notes on a meeting between your main character and another character that enters the room or space.

Chapter 3
Expressing the Story

There are two basic aspects to **Expressing a Story**:

Voicing the Story refers to how the story is told, i.e. what kind of narration is involved and whether the story is told as if it is happening now or has happened in the past.

Dialogue refers to the manner in which the speech of characters is conveyed in the story.

1. Voicing the Story

The **Voice** in the story is the person who tells the story.

The story can be told by the main character, or one of the other characters. It can be told by someone who has nothing to do with the characters, but relates events in an impartial way.

The story can also be told as if it happened sometime ago (Past Tense) or is happening right now (Present Tense).

Voicing a story involves the following:

Past Tense • **Present Tense**
First Person Narrator • **Third Person Narrator**

a. Past Tense

Most stories are told in the **Past Tense**. It allows the narrator to describe the events that happened, but also to reflect on them by offering insights and comments as the story progresses.

The first drafts of all the story openings so far have been given in the past tense. Most people find it easier to use the past tense because we are all used to relating past events to others.

Example: Find a short extract in the story ***The Farley Mill*** where an early part of the narrative is told in the past tense.

The Farley children had been brought up in the lap of luxury. Robert had just celebrated his eleventh birthday, and his sister, Emily, trailed him by just nine months. 1829 had been a cold year and, even by May, the sun had barely shone. The bleak Lancashire landscape, with its craggy and jutting hills, had seen no real spring that year; even the hardy plants had not yet flowered.

None of this mattered to the Farley children. Their existence was cosy: they lived in a beautiful, old, stone mansion, that nestled itself in a valley that had a fast-flowing river. In the distance, further downriver, existed a large factory. Carts and transports were constantly ferrying people to and from the factory, past the grand and conspicuous entrance of the Farley Mansion.

b. Present Tense

Present Tense is not so commonly used in the telling of stories, but it is a very effective device. The reason why many people find it difficult to write in present tense is they do not often use it in everyday speech.

However, when present tense is utilised it makes the story feel immediate, as if it is happening right now, at that very moment.

Present tense can also be used for part of a story. For example, it might be used for flashbacks or flashforwards to emphasise the change in time that has occurred.

The second drafts of all the story openings in this book have been given in the present tense to provide an opportunity to practise this skill.

Example: Find a short extract in ***The Music Box*** where the story is told in the present tense.

This is the opening of the story, told in present tense.

A family surrounds a four-poster bed in a dimly-lit room. There are sounds of weeping. A single candle burns on a table and lights the pale, feverish face of Alois who lies in bed. His breathing is faint and his wife, Josephine, holds his limp hand. All of a sudden, Alois attempts to lift himself up from the pillow.

He cough and rasps, "Josephine, bring Katrine to me." Josephine glances at a young girl of about 12 years of age with blonde plaited hair cowering in the corner of the room, then signals for her to approach. Katrine edges forward and other family members reluctantly part to let her through.

Alois pulls her close and gasps, "There's something I've never told you about my mother. Sonnenburgs are special and you..."

Josephine intervenes, "Shush, my dear, just rest.' He sinks back and his body goes into spasm. Josephine pushes Katrine away.

Exercise 3: 1

Continue this story opening called ***Jungle Explorer***. Try it first in the past tense and then write the same again in the present tense.

Past Tense Opening

Lesley crawled forward through the undergrowth. A dangerous snake slithered past her and for a moment she froze with fear. It was very hot and humid and the sweat ran from Lesley's forehead into her eyes making them smart.

Lesley parted the leaves of a giant bush. Was she seeing things? Lesley rubbed the sweat from her eyes. Before her lay the most amazing sight. It was the ancient lost city of the jungle. Suddenly, there was a movement up ahead. Lesley was not alone...

Present Tense Opening

Lesley crawls forward through the undergrowth. A dangerous snake slithers past her and for a moment she freezes with fear. It is very hot and humid and the sweat runs from Lesley's forehead into her eyes making them smart.

Lesley parts the leaves of a giant bush. Is she seeing things? Lesley rubs the sweat from her eyes. Before her lies the most amazing sight. It is the ancient lost city of the jungle. Suddenly, there is a movement up ahead. Lesley is not alone...

c. First Person Narration

A **First Person Narrator** tells the story as *'I'* or *'we'*. It is as if that person(s) is the one who is, or has, experienced the events of the story.

First person narration can seem personal and emotionally more engaging, as it closely links the reader to what is happening in the story from a particular point of view.

Contractions such as *'I'm'* in place of *'I am'*, etc. can be used as the character is relating their own story in the present tense.

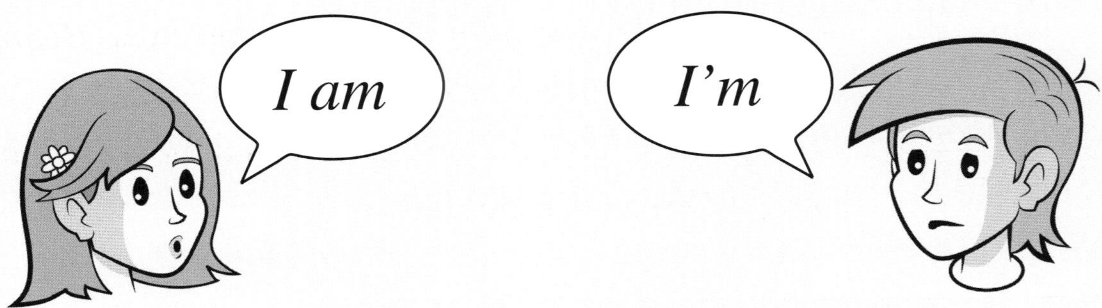

Some contractions work for the past tense, such as *'I'd'* in place of *'I had.'*

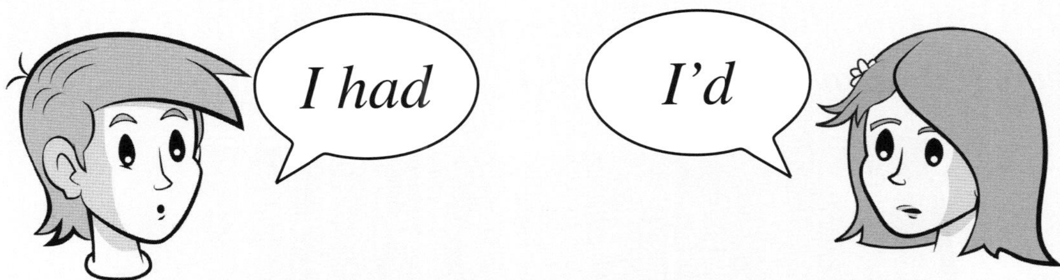

It overcomes one major disadvantage of telling the story in the past tense; we already know what the final outcome will be: the main character survived to tell the tale.

However, if the story is told in the present tense using first person narration, this problem does not occur. Everything is happening at that moment and no clue as to what might happen next is given. This makes the future a mystery.

Example: Write an extract of ***The History of Johnny Sweep***, using first person narration in present tense.

The History of Johnny Sweep has been written using third person narration in past tense.

However, the 'Writing in Role' exercise in the first chapter of this book was written using first person in present tense apart from Johnny's reflections on his past life.

Here is an extract from that exercise:

I have no idea how old I am. Since I have learnt to count up to ten, I worked out that it has been five summers and winters since Scratch, the master sweep, apprenticed me. He was nicknamed Scratch because that's just what he did; scratch himself all over. It is now the sixth winter and the local parish has made me over to Scratch fully and he owns me. For good measure, the parish threw in Toby, my little brother, too. Scratch says he will be a burden until he is old enough to sweep - just another mouth to feed. Not that there is ever enough food anyway.

Exercise 3: 2

Continue writing this story called ***Lost in the Desert.*** Write in the first person and in present tense.

The sun beats down mercilessly. I need water! My throat is so parched I can hardly swallow. I stumble forward down yet another sand dune and my legs almost give way under me. The desert stretches out as far as the eye can see.

It's hours since our light aircraft crashed. I'm the only survivor. All at once, I spot a circle of palm trees in the distance. It could be an oasis. Am I seeing things? Is it a mirage? I stagger onwards in hope...

c. Third Person Narration

Third Person Narration is when the pronoun **he**, **she**, **they** or **it** is used. The narrator is one step removed from the action and is able to stand outside the story and comment on what is happening and what every character is thinking.

Contractions of speech are not employed as regularly in third person narration, except when direct speech is used. This will depend on how formal or informal the writing style is.

This kind of narrator either knows the character, i.e. is a friend or relative, or is the silent voice of the author. They have extensive knowledge of the story world and speak from the point of view of the main character, sharing their thoughts and feelings.

This is sometimes called **Close Third Narration**. This form of narration can involve **Superior Position**, meaning the writer knows things outside of the situation that the hero does not know.

Example: Using an extract from ***The Farley Mill***, indicate the use of a third person narrator in past tense.

Mr Farley was a self-made man. He had come up the hard way. His parents had been just as poor as the people who now worked for him. He barely had any schooling and virtually all he knew was self-taught. Mr Farley gave no quarter and expected none. People were commodities to him – he had just

been lucky enough to escape the life they were experiencing. Although in his heart of hearts he did not really believe it was luck. To him it was stealth, determination and sheer force of will that had taken him from the gutter to being the owner of Farley Mill. He was often heard boasting to his wealthy and admiring friends, "The basis of my fortune is cheap labour – work them more – pay them less."

Ever since the children's mother had died a year earlier, the Farley children had been spoilt even more. Mr Farley focused all his attention on providing for their physical needs. This included many luxuries, although the children were so used to it, for them it was normality.

The children's lives were filled with toys, exquisite outfits and the choicest of foods. An extensive household comprising a cook, a housekeeper, three maids and a butler delivered all this but, most important of all, was the children's austere, but efficient nanny, Mrs Austin. However, nothing could replace the tender, loving care of a mother.

Exercise 3: 3

Try continuing this story opening from ***Sky High***. There is a choice between two scenarios; either write about a toppling crane or a skyscraper that is on fire.

1. ___Name___ *had been on shift since 8.00am that morning. He/she was due a tea break in ten minutes and was looking forward to being on solid ground again.*

Just when ___Name___ *was about to descend the crane's spiral stairwell there was a judder.* ___Name___ *felt the giant crane lurch slightly to the right. The crane's cab was five hundred feet above the ground. Would* ___Name___ *escape in time? He/she began to panic...*

or

2. *I really loved working in the highest office in the newest London skyscraper. That morning, I was busily completing my business acounts in my office.*

Suddenly, there was a loud boom that rocked the whole building. The telephone rang on my desk and security informed me that there was a raging fire engulfing the floor just below mine.

I immediately left the office and made for the fire escape. When I opened the fire door, flames leapt up from the staircase. I was desperate...

____

____

____

____

____

____

____

____

____

2. Dialogue

Dialogue is very important in stories because conversing is the main way in which characters interact. This reflects real life, as human beings constantly communicate through language.

Therefore a story that involves a number of characters would seem unnatural if no dialogue was ever used.

The conflicts and tensions between characters are mostly expressed through dialogue.

Dialogue can also give the reader very important insights about the motives of the main characters.

Creating effective story dialogue involves the following:

Indirect (Reported) Speech • Direct Speech
Direct Speech Introductions • Speech Patterns
Revealing Character

a. Indirect (Reported) Speech

Indirect or **Reported Speech** is a very important device for telling stories. **It occurs when the meaning of what someone has said or written is conveyed or put across without using the exact words.**

For example:
The boys said they were late because they were kept in school detention.
This sentence conveys the meaning, but does not use the exact words. **No speech marks are used.**

The exact words may have been:
"We're late because we were kept in school detention."
The use of speech marks indicates these were the exact words that were spoken.

Example: Demonstrate the effective use of indirect speech in ***The Farley Mill***.

Mr Farley talks to his children about many things. It is written as indirect speech as no actual words are recorded.

Every evening at dinner, Mr Farley felt obliged to fill his children's heads with facts about the textile business. They were told about production schedules, the cost of raw materials and the purchase of wool, and the transportation of coal to the works and its storage. Robert expressed an interest by questioning his father on such matters, particularly when the matter of steam engines was raised and how they powered the mill. However, although Emily was always polite, she was thoroughly bored by his talk.

Once this ritual was over, an even more trying one was endured by the children; Mr Farley would regale them on his own personal achievements. They listened to him speak of his rise from poverty to riches. He described the tiny house he had grown up in and promised to take the children there some day. His heart would be full of emotion

as he related every detail about his drunken father who would beat him for the slightest misdemeanour. This was all done to impress on the children how lucky they were to have a father who not only provided for them, but did not issue frequent beatings for their minor offences. By the end of every day, they were exhausted from having to listen to an endless diatribe of self-congratulatory personal history.

Exercise 3: 4

Think about ***The Tree House*** or ***Locked In*** again. Rewrite a short section of the story to include some indirect speech of the characters.

b. Direct Speech

Direct Speech allows the writer to record the exact words of each character.

Remember that conversations between characters should always have some level of conflict as this creates tension.

There are **six rules** for using direct speech:

1. Opening or closing comments should be separated from speech with a comma.
2. Use speech marks to open and close speech.
3. Always commence speech with a capital letter.
4. If there is a break in speech, but the same speaker then continues speaking and there is no full stop, a capital letter is not used.
5. A new line is used for every new speaker.
6. Indent the first line of speech, as if it is a new paragraph.

This example shows all six rules in operation.

"When are we going to the park?" Patricia questioned, "because I am beginning to feel very bored."

"Stop pestering me," her dad retorted, "your mother needs to take a rest. She has been working all day."

Dos and Don'ts in Direct Speech

1. Avoid too much speech - the worst kind of stories involve pages of dialogue.

A story is not a play, so the 'talking heads' scenario should be avoided. Stories are mainly narration.

Speech should be included when it helps develop the story and someone has something important to say.
E.g. a character might say, *"I'm asking you to listen very carefully while I explain the truth to you."* etc.

2. Always use conflict in direct speech - if there is no conflict there is no tension, and the reader will lose interest. E.g. *Michael laughed, "I thought you could read a map. We're lost, aren't we?"*

Rita gave him the map, "Here, see if you can do better, clever clogs."

Example: Demonstrate the effective use of direct speech in ***Florence Bovington Goes East***.

Florence meets up with Tilly in the garden for a discussion.

After attending church on Sunday and taking a rest, Florence took the air with Rose at 4.00pm precisely. Railings and privets surrounded the garden in the centre of the square. Rose unlocked the gate and was about to go in, but Florence indicated they should wait. Moments later, Tilly arrived wearing exactly the same outfit as before. Florence felt embarrassed and overdressed, as she was now wearing a lace brocade dress and a dark blue blouse.

"You look very fetchin', miss."

Florence smiled, even though she did not understand Tilly's slang, but somehow knew it was a compliment.

"You can call me Florence. Let's go in, Tilly."

Rose was intrigued by the kind of liaison Florence had struck up with Tilly, so she followed on behind at a listening distance.

Florence and Tilly strolled along the pathway for some time in silence. The birds sang, the roses were in full bloom and the willow trees created a tunnel-like effect as they overhung the path. The whole garden was a feast of colour, since the flowerbeds were graced with lilacs, tulips, and crocuses.

"This is lovely, miss... I mean... Florence."

"I do this every day about the same time."

Tilly was impressed, "Really, miss? Cor, you're lucky."

"Don't you ever take walks like this?"

Tilly looked sad, "I can't… miss… Florence."

Florence stopped, "Why not? London has parks."

"Don't have time. Works as a seamstress at Bluesdales. It's awful 'ard."

Florence felt sorry for Tilly, just as she had done on the first day she met her. She herself was so privileged and Tilly so deprived of the smallest luxury. Yet Tilly had a cheerfulness that Florence craved and longed for.

"Do you have friends, Tilly?"

"I don't have no friends to speak of, miss. I can call yer miss sometimes, rather than yer proper name, with you bein' so posh an' all?"

Florence nodded.

"Well, I s'pose there's Polly at the works, but she ain't really a proper friend. I talk to 'er sometimes though. Big girl, she is, with fat fingers. Finds the delicate stitchin' difficult 'cos of that. Mr Weedle ain't 'alf bad to 'er."

"Mr Weedle?"

"Yeah, 'e supervises us. Bad'n 'e is."

Florence stopped, reached across and touched Tilly's arm. They faced each other.

"Tilly, perhaps we could be friends?"

Tilly hung her head and looked embarrassed.

"Well?"

"You bein' friends with the likes of me, miss? I mean..."

Florence pressed in, "Why not, Tilly?"

Tilly's face lit up, "Well, if you be wantin' it, miss," then she looked downcast, as a more disturbing thought occurred to her, "but you don't have to take pity on me, miss, 'cos of me situation."

Exercise 3: 5

Think about ***The Tree House*** or ***Locked In***. Write a short conversation between the two characters using direct speech that involves friction or conflict.

c. Direct Speech Introductions

Direct speech can be introduced by using a verb or descriptive statement before or after the speech to indicate the way the speaker delivers the line.

Sometimes no introduction is needed if the line's meaning is clear and it is clear who is speaking at that moment.

Try to use verbs other than *'said'* or *'says'*. They are overused, so use them sparingly.

Here is a list of more interesting verbs:

advised; announced; answered; argued; asked; bellowed; boasted; bragged; called; continued; cried; declared; demanded; enquired; exclaimed; gabbled; growled; joked; lied; moaned; ordered; pleaded; repeated; replied; retorted; shouted; sobbed; spoke; screamed; stammered; stuttered; suggested; told; uttered; warned; whispered; yelled.

Example: Use ***The Music Box*** to indicate effective ways of introducing direct speech.

Katrine and her aunt clash severely.

Katrine interrupts, "My father taught me and said he would send me to the academy in Salzburg for an audition."

Aunt Eugene smirks, "Huh! Well I don't think you'll ever amount to anything."

Katrine retorts, "You played once, so why do you forbid me to play?"

"Enough!"

With a look of disdain on her face, Aunt Eugene turns and marches out the door, slamming it behind her.

Exercise 3: 6

Using ***The Tree House*** or ***Locked In***, rewrite a section of direct speech using different forms of introduction.

____

____

____

____

____

____

____

____

____

d. Speech Patterns

Here are two important things about the way people speak:

1. Contractions in Speech:

Most people use contractions in speech because it is quicker to say.

Occasionally a person might say something in full to make more impact or emphasise what they are saying.

For example, instead of saying in full: *"You are going to do as I say because I am your mother,"* someone will probably say, *"You're going to do as I say because I'm your mother."*

2. Styles of Speech:

English is spoken in many different styles and accents. This variety can be reflected in direct speech.

The way a person speaks can indicate age, gender, status, background, attitude, level of education, etc.

This can be illustrated in the following examples:

Formal and Educated Speech
E.g. *"Good morning, members of the jury. It is of utmost importance that you attempt to follow the details of the case before you, in order that you can reach a just verdict."*

Informal and Uneducated Speech
E.g. *"Nah, don't believe it's there. Yer lyin' ain't yer?"*

Foreign styles of Speech
E.g. *"What you say? I not speak English well."*

Impediments in Speech
E.g. *"P...p...p...perfect. I would n...n...now like to introduce G...G...Gertrude to all of you."*

Childlike Speech

E.g. *"Mummy, can we go to the shop to buy some sweeties? Please, please, I'll help forever and ever with everything."*

Clipped and Economical Speech

E.g. *"I said it once, listen!" There was a silence.*

Verbose and Long-winded Speech

E.g. *"I would like to start this important and significant yearly assembly by congratulating all the school staff one by one for their dedicated hard work. After I have done this at length, I will give out the prizes to the children and say as much as I can about each one of our 50 prize winners."*

There are many more ways speech can be formulated. As characters are developed in a story the way they speak can become more obvious to the writer.

Authors try to imagine their characters speaking and often base the speech patterns of characters upon people that they know.

Example: Demonstrate the effective use of two different speech patterns in ***Florence Bovington Goes East*** by using an extract from the story.

There is a big contrast between the way Florence speaks and the manner in which Tilly expresses herself. Florence speaks standard English, but Tilly uses a Cockney dialect.

Tilly drew out a postcard from her apron.

"Seein' as you're me special friend, I'd like to show you this."

Florence took the card. It was a sea view.

"See on the back, miss, are some words. Me aunt sent it me when she 'ad a day out there. Can't read it though."

"You don't read?" Florence questioned.

"Only a couple of words."

Florence read, "To Tilly, having a lovely day here. The sun is shining and the sea is very blue. Love, Aunty Annie."

Exercise 3: 7

Think about ***The Tree House*** or ***Locked In*** again. Rewrite a conversation between the two characters to indicate they have different speech patterns.

e. Revealing Character

The things people say and how they say them reveal very important things about a person's character and what motivates them.

Supertext is the actual words a person says, e.g. *"I really like you. You're so clever. Did you do the homework?"*

Subtext is the hidden meaning behind the words, e.g. *"Actually, I loathe you really, but I'm going to say I like you because I want to copy all your homework."*

Subtext is like an iceberg. The supertext (actual words) are one-eighth of the iceberg and can be seen on the surface. The subtext (hidden meanings) are seven-eighths of the iceberg and this is below the surface.

The subtext is not stated, but might be implied in the tone of voice, the look in someone's eye or a gesture.

It is very important in writing to describe the hidden thoughts and motivations of characters as this is of great interest to the reader.

Subtext can be conveyed through the tone of the voice, a display or emotion, or gestures and body language.

Dramatic Irony or Double Meanings

Supertext and subtext in speech means that all dialogue has the potential to have **Double Meanings**. One thing is said but something else is meant.

A double meaning in the text is called **Dramatic Irony**. When present, it creates very strong emotional reactions in a reader, ranging from anger on the one hand to humour on the other.

Human beings are always interested in the deeper meaning of what a character might be saying, rather than the plain words.

Humour can be created by revealing thoughts to the reader that contrast strongly with what is being said by the speaker:

Trudy listened to Lara mimic her favourite popstar. She thought to herself, 'Lara can't sing.'

"Wow!" Trudy enthused. "That's really good."

Trudy hoped that would be the end of the painful rendering of the song, but Lara just kept going. Even worse, she started to dance.

Trudy forced a smile, "You are really... well, like her."

"Really?" Lara said excitedly.

'No,' Trudy thought privately; Lara was out of tune, sang like a strangled cat and, worst of all, she had absolutely no idea of how awful her singing actually was. Finally, to Trudy's relief, she finished.

Lara smiled, "Shall I sing you another?"

Anger can also be generated in the reader by showing the character is acting with deceitful, nasty or evil intentions.

Ryan opened the largest Christmas present first. He was hoping for a train set. Instead, it was a boring board game his parents thought he wanted. 'Why didn't they listen?' he thought.

Ryan muttered, "Oh, that's nice."

His brother, Peter, tore the wrapping paper off his present and it was the very train set that Ryan had wanted. He couldn't believe it. How could his parents give his little brother the best present?

Ryan watched Peter start to assemble the track; he was having difficulty piecing it together.

"I'll help. Let me take a look," Ryan offered.

Ryan made sure Peter couldn't see what he was doing. He snapped one length of the track in two. He turned back to Peter.

"Sorry, it just broke in my hand."

Peter started to cry, but Ryan felt pleased with himself. However, unbeknown to Ryan, his parents had noted his actions with alarm.

Example: **Demonstrate the use of subtext in *The Farley Mill*.**

The Farley children, Robert and Emily are grieving over the loss of their mother and are feeling uncared for because of their father's lack of interest in them on a personal level.

Both characters are angry and hurt by this, but their father refuses to discuss how they really feel and bans all talk of their late mother.

As a result, Robert and Emily bicker and quarrel all the time. They take out their anger and frustration on each other. This means that anything they say to each other is really an expression of anger about their family situation.

A month passes. Spring has finally arrived, although the sense of gloom in the Farley household has not lifted. The children still bicker every day about anything and everything, particularly when it comes to play.

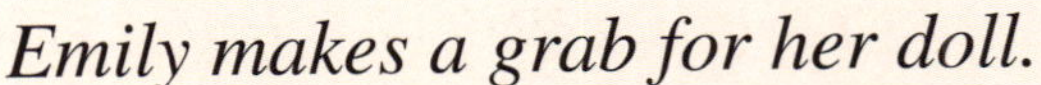

Emily makes a grab for her doll.

"You always take my things."

"Don't be so quarrelsome, sister," Robert taunts.

"It's Emily! Mother said you have to use people's names."

"Sister Emily then."

Emily snatches the doll from Robert's hands and a leg comes off and falls to the floor.

Robert sniggers.

"You're horrible. Now Patsy won't be able to walk anymore."

"It's just a doll."

Emily cries.

The door flings open and Mrs Austin enters.

"Quarrelling again? Now children, why can't you play nicely?"

Robert protests, "She only wants to do girly things. I want some adventure."

Robert slips out a lead soldier from his pocket. He carefully places the red-uniformed grenadier on the table and views it from eye-level. His eyes widen with excitement as he starts to make gunfire noises.

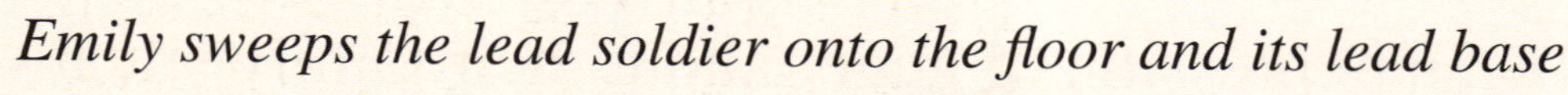

Emily sweeps the lead soldier onto the floor and its lead base breaks off. "There, that'll teach you!"

Robert rushes at Emily and tries to grab her hair, but Mrs Austin intervenes. She seizes both children by the lapels and pulls them apart, as their arms whizz around in an attempt to land blows.

Emily screams, "Beastly boy!"

Robert yells with rage, "You broke my favourite soldier."

Both children descend into tears and sobs.

"This is no way for a young gentleman or a young lady to behave."

Mrs Austin guides each child to a chair in turn, and forces them to sit.

"Now, you'll both say sorry, or your father will hear of this."

Emily heaves, "I'll never say sorry."

"Me neither!"

Exercise 3: 8

Think about ***The Tree House*** or ***Locked In*** again. Rewrite some dialogue between characters and ensure it now has subtext or deeper meanings.

Your Own Story - Draft Two

Now write your own story using one of the following scenarios. There are two story scenarios to choose from:

Story 1 - ***The Tree House*** or **Story 2** - ***Locked In***

Write Story 1 or 2 in this book. Once you have learnt the principles, you can write the other story.

Try and include ideas and techniques from chapters 2 and 3.

Chapter 2 - Story Texture and Dynamics

1. Story Texture

This involves the following components:

- mood, atmosphere, intrigue or curiosity and surprise

2. Story Dynamics

This involves the following components:

- tension, suspense, anticipation and conflict

Chapter 3 - Expressing the Story

1. Voicing the Story

This refers to how the story is told:

- past or present tense and first or third person narrator

2. Story Dialogue

This refers to how speech is conveyed:

- indirect (reported) speech, direct speech, use of direct speech introductions, speech patterns and the use of subtext to reveal character

Observe these Rules and complete the Story

1. The character is not allowed to leave the space. Find a way to end the story in the space without leaving it.
2. One other character can enter the space and leave it at some point in the story.
3. Write out the scenario first and then continue the story.

Second Draft - Story 1

The Tree House

Opening Scenario in Present Tense:

I had climbed the ladder to the tree house some hours before and pulled it up behind me. Now I am safe - well for now anyway. I had built the tree house the previous summer and it is my only place of refuge. It has been a terrifying day. But now nobody knows where I am; at least I hope so. There are a few meagre supplies of food I have stored in the corner. I look out of the small opening that serves as a window and wonder what will happen next...

Second Draft - Story 2

Locked In

Opening Scenario in Present Tense:

I try the front door in the flat but it is locked. Then I go to the windows but they are all sealed. I take out a penknife and dig away at the seals until they give way. I look out, but I am four storeys up. The new landlord has put bars on the opening to stop anybody desperate enough to jump. Who has locked me in and why? I go back to the door and thump on it as hard as I can. Silence. There is a telephone on the coffee table. I pick up the receiver. It is dead. I have no mobile phone or any other of my belongings with me. What am I going to do?

Choose to write either **Story 1** or **Story 2**, then use the Planning page to write down some ideas for your story.

Planning - 2nd Draft

Story 1 - *The Tree House*

or Story 2 - *Locked In*

Let's plan a second draft.

Write the 2nd draft of ***The Tree House*** or ***Locked In***. Copy out the opening scenario on Story Page 1, 2nd draft then continue your story on the following pages.

Story Page 1 - 2nd Draft

The Tree House or ***Locked In***

Shock

Story Page 2 - 2nd Draft

The Tree House **or** ***Locked In***

Intrigue

Story Page 3 - 2nd Draft

The Tree House or ***Locked In***

Concern

Story Page 4 - 2nd Draft

The Tree House or ***Locked In***

Fright

Story Page 5 - 2nd Draft

The Tree House **or** ***Locked In***

Panic

Story Page 6 - 2nd Draft

The Tree House or ***Locked In***

Scores Out of Ten	Spelling & Grammar →		Creativity →	

Marking the Stories

If you are working with a teacher, tutor or an experienced adult the stories can be given a Creativity and a Spelling & Grammar mark.

Mark Scheme (marks 1 to 10)

Outstanding	**10 marks**	*Acceptable*	**5 marks**
Excellent	**9 marks**	*Needs some work*	**4 marks**
Very Good	**8 marks**	*Needs a lot of work*	**3 marks**
Good	**7 marks**	*Requires more effort*	**2 marks**
Satisfactory	**6 marks**	*Rework it completely*	**1 mark**

A mark below **5** means the story should be attempted again.

	Spelling & Grammar	Creativity
Story 1 - **The Tree House** *First Draft*		
Story 2 - **Locked In** *First Draft*		
Story 1 - **The Tree House** *Second Draft*		
Story 2 - **Locked In** *Second Draft*		

Total Score + **Total Score**

Average Score
out of 10
(Divide total by 8)

Overall Percentage

%

Total Score

CERTIFICATE OF

ACHIEVEMENT

This certifies

____

has successfully completed

KS2 Creative Writing
Year 5
WORKBOOK **1**

Overall percentage score achieved [ ] %

Comment ______________________________

____

Signed ______________________________
(teacher/parent/guardian)

Date ______________________________